DENNIS J. SPORRE

THE CREATIVE IMPULSE
An Introduction to the Arts

A Custom Edition

Taken from:
The Creative Impulse: An Introduction to the Arts, Sixth Edition
by Dennis J. Sporre

PEARSON
Custom Publishing

PEARSON
Prentice Hall

Cover Art: *Promise #17*, by Antoinette M. Winters.

Taken from:

The Creative Impulse, Sixth Edition
by Dennis J. Sporre
Copyright © 2003, 2000, 1996, 1993, 1990, 1987 by Prentice-Hall, Inc.
A Pearson Education Company
Upper Saddle River, New Jersey 07458

This special edition published in cooperation with Pearson Custom Publishing.

Printed in the United States of America

10 9 8 7

ISBN 0-536-91275-0

2005120012

DG/JM

Please visit our web site at *www.pearsoncustom.com*

PEARSON CUSTOM PUBLISHING
75 Arlington Street, Suite 300, Boston, MA 02116
A Pearson Education Company

Getting Started and Understanding and Evaluating the Arts

GETTING STARTED AND UNDERSTANDING AND EVALUATING THE ARTS

OUTLINE

GETTING STARTED

TWO-DIMENSIONAL ART
TECHNIQUES: Linear Perspective

SCULPTURE
TECHNIQUES: Lost-Wax Casting

ARCHITECTURE

MUSIC
TECHNIQUES: Musical Notation

THEATRE

LITERATURE

FILM

DANCE

FEATURES

UNDERSTANDING AND EVALUATING THE ARTS

PUTTING THE ARTS IN CONTEXT

THE ARTS AND WAYS OF KNOWING
■ What Concerns Art?
  Creativity
  Aesthetic Communication
  Symbols
  Fine and Applied Art

THE FUNCTIONS OF ART
■ Entertainment
■ Political and Social
  Commentary
■ Therapy
■ Artifact

EVALUATING WORKS OF ART
■ Types of Criticism
■ Making Judgments

0.1 Antonio Canova, Perseus Holding the Head of Medusa, 1804–08. Marble, 7 ft 2⅝ ins (2.20 m) high. The Metropolitan Museum of Art, New York (Fletcher Fund) 1967.

GETTING STARTED

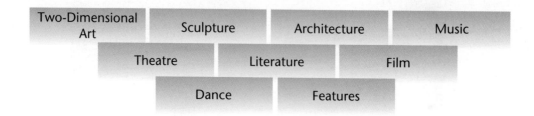

Getting Started takes us into the land of basic terminology and fundamental artistic concepts. In other words, we are about to sample some of the things that will help us to identify and communicate important characteristics appropriate to the works of two-dimensional art, sculpture, music, theatre, dance, literature, and film that are presented later in the text.

Although it may not seem so on first reading, the terms and concepts discussed here represent only a fraction of what we might study. The terms are technical, and, undoubtedly, you will want to return to this section as you encounter works of art in the chapters that follow, especially when you seek to describe and compare paintings, musical selections, and so on, using accurate terminology.

Two-Dimensional Art

Two-dimensional art consists of paintings, drawings, prints, and photographs, which differ from each other primarily in the technique of their execution. Probably, our initial response to all four is a response to content—that is, we first notice what the painting, drawing, print, or photogaph seems to be about. Such recognition usually triggers an emotional and intellectual response that leads us into the work's meaning. Beyond the recognition of content, however, lie the technical elements chosen by artists to make their vision appear the way they wish it to appear, and these include **media** and **composition**.

Media

The media of the two-dimensional arts are paintings, drawings, prints, and photography. Paintings and drawings can be executed with oils, watercolors, tempera, acrylics, ink, and pencils, to name just a few of the more obvious. Each physical medium has its own particular characteristics. As an example, let us look at *oils.*

Oils, developed around the beginning of the fifteenth century, offer artists a broad range of color possibilities; they do not dry quickly and can, therefore, be reworked; they present many options for textural manipulation; and they are durable. Look at the texture in the brushwork of Van Gogh's (van-GOH or van GAHK) *Harvest at La Crau* (see Fig. **16.20**). This kind of manipulation is a characteristic of oil. Whatever the physical medium—that is, painting, drawing, print, or photograph—we can find identifiable characteristics that shape the final work of art. Had the artist chosen a different physical medium, the work—all other things being equal—would not look the same.

Composition

The second area that we can isolate and respond to involves artists' use of the *elements* and *principles of composition.* These make up the building blocks of two-dimensional works of art. Among others, these elements and principles include **line**, **form**, **color**, **repetition**, and **balance**.

Elements

The primary element of composition is line. In Joan Miró's (hoh-AHN mee-ROH) *Composition* (Fig. **0.2**) we see amorphous shapes. Some of these are like cartoon

figures—identifiable because of their outline—but the other shapes also exemplify line, and they do so because they create boundaries between areas of color and between other shapes or forms. Essentially, line is either curved or straight, and it is used by artists to control our vision and to create unity, emotional value, and, ultimately, meaning.

Form and line are closely related. Form as a compositional element is the **shape** of an object. It is the space described by line. A building is a form. So is a tree. We perceive them as buildings or trees, and we perceive their individual details, because of the line by which they are composed. *Color* is a somewhat complex compositional element. The word **hues** is used to describe the basic colors of the spectrum (Fig. 0.3). The apparent whiteness or grayness of a color is its **value** (Fig. 0.4). When we observe a work of art, we can, among other aspects of color, identify, respond to, and describe the breadth of the *palette*—how many different hues and values the artist has used—and the way the artist has used those hues and values.

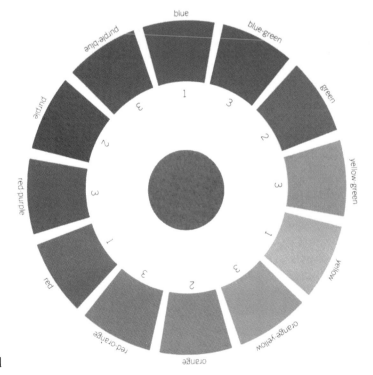

0.3 Color wheel.

☐ White		☐ W	
☐ High Light		☐ HL	☐ Yellow
☐ Light	Yellow-green ☐	☐ L	☐ Yellow-orange
☐ Medium Light	Green ☐	☐ ML	☐ Orange
☐ Medium (grey)	Blue-green ☐	☐ M	☐ Red-orange
■ High dark	Blue ☐	☐ MD	☐ Red
■ Dark	Blue-violet ☐	☐ D	☐ Red-violet
■ Low dark	Violet ☐	☐ LD	
■ Black		☐ B	

0.4 Value scale.

Principles

The principles of composition include *repetition* (the way in which the elements of the picture are repeated or alternated) and *balance* (the way in which the picture stands on its axes). In Picasso's (pee-KAH-soh) *Girl Before a Mirror* (Fig. 0.6), the artist has ordered the recurrence of elements in a regular manner. He has placed hard angles and soft curves side by side, and, in addition, has used two geometric forms, the oval and the diamond, over and over again to build up the forms of the work. He also has balanced the picture with nearly identical shapes on each side of the central axis. When shapes and colors that are identical appear on either side of the axis, it creates a condition called **symmetry**. Balance achieved by using unequal shapes, as demonstrated in Figures **0.2** and **0.6**, indicates asymmetry, the balancing of unlike objects—also known as psychological balance. If the repeated elements are of the same size or importance, then the repetition is called regular. If they are of differing size and/or importance, then the repetition is called irregular.

TECHNIQUES
▪ Linear Perspective ▪

Throughout the text, we will witness how two-dimensional artists utilize "deep space"—that is, the illusion of depth in their works. One of the methods for creating deep space that appears rational or **naturalistic** is the use of **linear perspective** (Fig. 0.5). Very simply, *linear perspective* is the creation of the illusion of distance in a two-dimensional artwork through the convention of line and foreshortening— that is, the illusion that parallel lines come together in the distance. Linear perspective is also called *scientific, mathematical one-point,* or *Renaissance perspective* and was developed in fifteenth-century Italy (see Chapter 10). It uses mathematical formulas to construct illusionistic images in which all elements are shaped by imaginary lines called *orthogonals* that converge in one or more *vanishing points* on a *horizon line*. Linear perspective is the system most people in the Euro-American cultures think of as perspective, because it is the visual code they are accustomed to seeing.

0.5 Linear perspective.

0.6 Pablo Picasso, *Girl Before a Mirror*, 1932. Oil on canvas, 64 × 51¼ ins (162.3 × 130.2 cm). Collection, Museum of Modern Art, New York (Gift of Mrs. Simon Guggenheim). Photo: © 1998 The Museum of Modern Art, New York. © Succession Picasso/DACS 2001.

Sculpture

Sculpture is a medium of three dimensions. Thus, in addition to those qualities of composition just noted, we can approach sculpture by another element of composition called **mass**: the size, shape, and volume of the forms. Sculpture appeals to us by how large or small it is and by the appearance of weight and density in its materials.

Dimensionality

As we have noted, sculpture defines actual space. Sculpture may be **full-round**, **relief**, or **linear**. Full-round works are freestanding and fully three-dimensional. They are meant to be viewed from any angle. Relief sculpture projects from a background and cannot be seen from all sides. It maintains a two-dimensional quality, as compared to full-rounded sculpture. Linear sculpture emphasizes construction with thin, tubular items such as wire or neon tubing.

Texture

The surface treatment (called texture) of a work of sculpture is as important as its dimensionality. Michelangelo carved *David* (see Fig. **11.24**) from marble, but he made the stone seem alive and warm like living flesh by giving it a lustrous, polished texture.

TECHNIQUES

▮ LOST-WAX CASTING ▮

The **lost-wax** technique, sometimes known by the French term *cire-perdue*, is a method of casting sculpture in which the basic mold is created by using a wax model, which is then melted to leave the desired spaces in the mold. The technique probably began in Egypt. By 200 B.C.E., the technique was used in China and ancient Mesopotamia, and it was used soon after that by the Benin people of Africa. It spread to Greece sometime in the late sixth century B.C.E.

The drawings indicated in Figure **0.7** illustrate the steps Benin sculptors would have utilized. A heat-resistant "core" of clay—approximately the shape of the sculpture—was covered by a layer of wax approximately the thickness of the final work. The sculptor carved the details in the wax. Rods and a pouring cup made of wax were attached to the model, and then the model, rods, and cup were covered with thick layers of clay. When the clay was dry, the mold was heated to melt the wax. Molten metal could then be poured into the mold. When the molten metal had dried, the clay mold was broken and removed, which meant that the sculpture could not be duplicated.

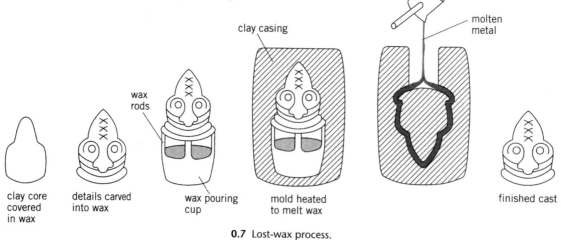

clay casing

molten metal

wax rods

clay core covered in wax

details carved into wax

wax pouring cup

mold heated to melt wax

finished cast

0.7 Lost-wax process.

Architecture

Architecture is often described as the art of sheltering, and it is the one art form that combines aesthetic considerations with intensely practical ones. Our formal responses to architecture often involve the purpose of the building: a church, an office building, a residence, and so on. The way architects merge interior function with exterior form provides much of our encounter with works of architecture.

Although a variety of fundamental technical elements exist in architecture, we will only discuss one: *structure*.

Structure

Architecture contains many systems of structure. As we travel through the centuries in our examination of human creativity, we will see examples of **post-and-lintel**, **cantilever**, **arch**, bearing wall, and skeleton frame structures. Laying horizontal pieces (**lintels**) across vertical supports (posts) gives us one of our oldest structural

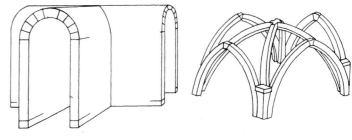

0.8 Groin vault.

0.9 Ribbed vault.

systems—that is, post-and-lintel (see Fig. **4.22**). When unimpeded interior space became an architectural necessity, the arch gave architects an additional means of solving the practical problems involved. Whether it was used in **vaults** (arches joined end to end) or in domes (concentric arches), as we shall see in the great Gothic cathedrals of the Middle Ages or the dome of the Pantheon (see Fig. **4.21**), the arch opened interior space to usable proportions. When vaults cross at right angles, they create a **groin vault** (Fig. **0.8**). The protruding masonry that indicates a diagonal juncture of arches in a tunnel vault is a **ribbed vault** (Fig. **0.9**). Cantilever, as exemplified in the Zarzuela (zahr-ZWAY-luh) Race Track (Fig. **0.10**), provided architects with dramatic means for expression, for here, unsupported, overhanging precipices define space.

0.10 Eduardo Torroja, Grandstand, Zarzuela Race Track, Madrid, 1935.

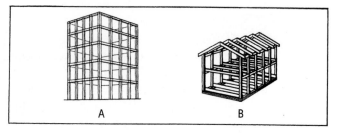

0.11 Skeleton frame structures: A. *Steel-Cage Construction*; B. *Balloon Construction*.

thus forming an exterior skin. When skeleton framing makes use of wood, as in house construction, the technique is called *balloon construction*. When metal forms the frame, as in skyscrapers, the technique is known as steel-cage construction (Fig. **0.11**).

The system of *bearing wall* has had ancient and modern applications. In it, the wall supports itself, the floors, and the roof, and both log cabins and solid masonry buildings are examples in which the wall is the structure. When the wall material is continuous (not joined or pieced together) it is called **monolithic**.

Finally, *skeleton frame* structure uses a framework to support the building. The walls are attached to the frame,

Music

Genres

Listening to music often begins with genre identification, simply because it helps us to know exactly what kind of

---

TECHNIQUES

▮ MUSICAL NOTATION ▮

Musical notation is a system of writing music so the composer can communicate clearly to the performer the pitches and rhythms (among other things) of the piece. A brief familiarity with this method of communication is important because later in the text we will illustrate characteristics of musical compositions with written notation.

The pitches of music are indicated with symbols, called *notes*, placed on a *staff*—five parallel lines on which each line and space represent a pitch (Fig. **0.12A**). The higher a note's placement on the staff, the higher the pitch. Seven of the twelve pitches of an octave in Western music are named after the first seven letters of the alphabet: A, B, C, D, E, F, G. The remaining five tones are indicated by the use of two signs, the *sharp* sign (♯) and the *flat* sign (♭) (Fig. **0.12B**). A *clef* (in French, "key") is placed at the beginning of the staff to show the pitch of each line and space (Figs. **0.12C** and **D**). Music is written in different *keys*—each associated with the presence of a central note, scale, and chord—which are indicated by a *key signature* (Figs. **0.12E** and **F**). *Rhythms* are indicated with notes indicating time values relative to each other (Fig. **0.12G**). The duration of silences in a musical piece is indicated by a symbol called a *rest* (Fig. **0.12H**).

0.12 Musical notation.

composition we are hearing. Being aware that we are listening to a **symphony**—a large musical composition for orchestra, typically consisting of four separate sections called "movements"—provides us with clues that are different from a **mass**—a choral setting of the Roman Catholic service, the Mass. A **concerto** (kahn-CHAIR-toh), a composition for solo instrument with accompaniment, gives us different experiences from an **opera** or **oratorio**, a large-scale choral work such as Handel's *Messiah* performed in concert form.

Melody and Form

Whatever the generic category, all music employs the same technical elements, of which **melody** and form are perhaps the two most obvious. We will introduce others at appropriate points in the text.

Melody is a succession of sounds with rhythmic and tonal organization. Any combination of musical tones constitutes a melody, but melody usually has particular qualities beyond being a mere succession of sounds. Musical ideas, for example, come to us in melodies called **themes**; shorter versions, brief melodic or rhythmic ideas, are called **motives** or **motifs** (moh-TEEF).

Form, like the principles of composition in visual art, gives musical compositions shape and organization. Composers use form to arrange musical elements and relationships into successive events or sections. Basically, we can listen for two types of form: *closed* and *open*. Closed forms direct our attention back into the composition by restating at the end of a thematic section the element that formed the beginning. This pattern of development often is described as ABA or AABA. The letters stand for specific thematic sections. Open form, on the other hand, uses repetition of thematic material as a departure point for further development, and the composition ends without repeating the opening section.

Theatre

The word "theatre" comes from the Greek word *theatron* (THAY-uh-trahn): the area of the Greek theatre building where the audience sat. Its literal meaning is "a place for seeing." Like the other **performing arts**, theatre is an interpretive discipline, because between the playwright and the audience stand the director, the designers, and the actors.

Genres

As in music, our enjoyment of theatre can be enhanced by understanding the genre—that is, the type of play—from which the performance evolves. We are probably most familiar with the genres of **tragedy** and **comedy**, but there are others.

We commonly describe a tragedy as a play with an unhappy ending, and typically, tragic heroes make free choices that cause suffering and defeat or sometimes triumph out of defeat. Often, the hero—the *protagonist*—undergoes a struggle that ends disastrously. In many respects, comedy is much more complex than tragedy and even harder to define. Comedy embraces a wide range of theatrical approaches, and when it is defined in its broadest terms, comedy may not even involve laughter. Although we can say, probably with some accuracy, that humor forms the root of all comedy, many comedies employ satire, and comedies often treat serious themes while remaining basically lighthearted in spirit.

These and the other genres of theatre guide our expectations as we witness a production. If we know the genre in advance, our responses move according to those expectations. If we do not know the genre, we have to work it out as the production unfolds.

Plot, Character, Thought, and Visual Elements

Technically, theatrical productions are shaped to a large degree by *plot*—that is, the structure of the play—the skeleton that gives it shape. The plot determines how a play works—how it moves from one moment to another, how conflicts are structured, and, ultimately, how the play comes to an end.

Plays also turn on *character*: the motivating psychological makeup of the people in the play. Although many plays focus on visual elements such as settings, lighting, and costumes, we find theatre engrossing because of the way plays reflect human behavior and conflict in human decisions and actions. Thus, when we attend a performance of a play, our primary attention focuses on how dialogue reveals character and how actors portray actions. Most plays hinge on the actions and decisions of one major character, called the *protagonist*, and when we follow his or her development and the consequences of his or her actions, we are led to an understanding of the play's meaning.

The meaning of the play—sometimes called its *thought*—like the meaning of any work of art, reveals what artists are trying to communicate to us about our universe.

The visual elements of a play comprise a number of factors including the relationship of the audience to the acting area—for example, the arena form in which the audience surrounds the stage area. Visual elements also include scenery, costumes, lighting, and actor movement.

Literature

Literature operates through a system of language in which the words themselves trigger our understanding.

Genres

Like many of the other arts, we approach literature first through the formal door of its genres. These are fiction, poetry, biography, and essay.

Fiction is a work created from the author's imagination rather than from fact. Normally, it takes one of two approaches to its subject matter: realistic—the appearance of observable, true-to-life details—or nonrealistic—fantasy. Other literary forms, such as narrative poetry, however, can also be fiction, and fictional elements can be introduced into forms such as biography and epic poetry. Traditionally, fiction is divided into novels and short stories.

Poetry, on the other hand, is a type of work designed to convey a vivid and imaginative sense of experience. It uses concentrated language, selected for its sound, suggestive power, and meaning, and employs specific technical devices such as meter, rhyme, and metaphor. Poetry can be divided into three major types: *narrative*, which tells a story, *dramatic*, which utilizes dramatic form or technique, and **lyric**, which consists of brief, subjective treatments employing strong imagination, melody, and feeling to create a single, unified, and intense impression of the personal emotion of the poet.

Over the centuries, *biography*, a written account of a person's life, has taken many forms, including literary narratives, simple catalogues of achievement, and psychological portraits. Biographies of saints and other religious figures are called hagiographies.

Traditionally, the *essay* is a short literary composition on a single subject, usually presenting the personal views of the author. Essays include many subforms and a variety of styles, but they uniformly present a personal point of view with a conscious attempt to achieve grace of expression.

Characteristically, the best essays are marked by clarity, good humor, wit, urbanity, and tolerance.

Point of View, Character, and Plot

In writing fiction, authors usually employ one of four *points of view*: (1) first person; (2) epistolary (the use of letters written by the characters); (3) third person; or (4) stream of consciousness (wherein a flow of thoughts and feelings comes from a specific character's psyche).

As in theatre, *character* also represents an important focus. The people in the work and their struggles with some important human problem give literature much of its appeal.

Plot in a work of literature may be a major or subordinate focus. Like theatrical plots, literary plots unfold the structure of the work and may come to a climax and resolution or leave the characters in a convenient place, allowing us to imagine their future lives continuing as their characters dictate.

Theme and Language

Most good stories have a dominant idea or *theme* by which the other elements are shaped. Although some critics argue that the quality of a theme is less important than what the author does with it, the best artworks are often those in which the author has taken a meaningful theme and developed it exceptionally.

In poetry, *language* that includes imagery—figures, which take words beyond their literal meaning, and **metaphors**, which give new implication to words—also provides an important focus.

Film

A product of modern technology, film brings us into a world that, apart from a lack of three-dimensionality, is often mistaken for reality. We are most familiar with the *narrative* film—that is, one that tells a story, such as the films directed by Alfred Hitchcock (Fig. 0.13). Two other types of film also exist—documentary film and absolute film. *Documentary* film is an attempt to record actuality, using either a sociological or a journalistic approach, and it

0.13 Alfred Hitchcock (director), *North by Northwest*, 1959. 136 minutes, MGM Studios, USA.

is normally not reenacted by professional actors but shot as the event occurs. *Absolute* film is film that exists for its own sake, for its record of movement or form. It does not use narrative techniques—although documentary techniques can be used in some instances. Created neither in the camera nor on location, absolute film is built carefully, piece by piece, on the editing table or through special effects and multiple-printing techniques.

Dance

Dance deals with the human form in time and space. In general, it follows one of three traditions: ballet, modern dance, and folk dance. *Ballet* comprises what can be called classical or formal dance; it is rich in tradition and rests heavily on a set of prescribed movements and actions. In general, ballet is a highly theatrical dance presentation consisting of solo dancers, duets, and choruses, or *corps de ballet* (kohr duh ba-LAY). According to the *Dance Encyclopedia*, ballet's basic principle is "the reduction of human gesture to bare essentials, heightened and developed into meaningful patterns."

Modern dance is a label given to a broad variety of highly individualized dance works limited to the twentieth and twenty-first centuries, essentially American in derivation, and antiballetic in philosophy. The basic principle of modern dance probably could be stated as an emphasis on natural and spontaneous or uninhibited movement in strong contrast with the conventionalized and specified movement of the ballet. Although narrative elements often exist in modern dance, the form emphasizes them less than does traditional ballet. Modern dance also differs significantly from ballet in its use of the human body and interaction with the dance floor.

Folk dance, somewhat like folk music, comprises a body of group dances performed to traditional music. As in folk music, the creator (in this case, the *choreographer*) remains unknown. Folk dance began as a necessary or formative part of various cultures with characteristics identifiable with a given culture. Folk dances developed over a period of years, passing from one generation to another. Each folk dance has its prescribed movements, rhythms, music, and costumes. At its core, folk dancing establishes an individual sense of participation in a society, tribe, or mass movement, and strengthens individuals' sense of belonging through collective dancing. On the other hand, however, folk dance often takes on the characteristics of concert dance—as many tourists can relate.

Line, Form, and Repetition

The compositional elements of line, form, and repetition apply to the human body in dance in exactly the same manner as they apply to painting and sculpture. As in all artworks occupying space, dance can create meaning by using horizontal line to suggest placidity, vertical line to suggest grandeur, and diagonal line to suggest movement. Dancers' bodies become like sculptures in motion as they move from one pose to another, and, because dancers move through time, the element of repetition serves a vital part of how choreographers put dances together and how we respond to them. Patterns of shapes and movement occur, and through them, like themes and variations in music, we find structure and meaning in dance works.

Features

Pronunciation

Throughout the text, whenever a name or term (whose pronunciation may be problematical) appears for the first time, a pronunciation guide follows immediately in parentheses. The stressed syllable appears in capital letters. The vowel and consonant selections to guide you in pronouncing the word are straightforward. The only usage that may be questionable is the use of the letter Y to suggest a long I sound—for example, the first person pronoun "I" would appear "Y," and the word "aisle" would appear "YL."

Profiles

Profile boxes appear throughout the text in order to draw our attention to the biography of a prominent person in the chapter. Profile boxes give us a chance to get to know these people a little better, spending more time with them than regular treatment in the text might allow.

Technology

Throughout history, humans have made discoveries and then turned those discoveries into tools or other useful devices that enhance the quality of life. As the text suggests, being a human being isn't much different today from what it was thousands of years ago. On the other hand, the nature of our world, as the result of our technological advancement, is considerably different. Thus, in each chapter we have a feature box to highlight some important technology that developed during the time covered in that chapter.

Masterwork

In a text such as this, which discusses nearly a thousand works of art in painting, sculpture, architecture, theatre, literature, dance, music, and film, we need occasionally to rest, to draw away from the flow of the material, and focus on a single, significant work of art. That is the purpose of the Masterwork boxes in each chapter. The presence of one particular work of art singled out as a Masterwork does not necessarily mean it is any better than the other works which have not been so designated.

The works selected are "masterworks" by whatever criteria we wish to define that term, but the selection is not intended as a hierarchical ranking system.

Focal Point

At the conclusion of each chapter a "Focal Point" section appears. Here we take the time to isolate a group of works, a special time, a combination of artists, or a locale that represents some important facet of the preceding chapter. In a way, the Focal Point section serves as a summary, because the material has a representative quality. Nonetheless, it is complete in itself, and we might even think that it belongs in the body of the chapter itself.

A Dynamic World

The boxes in each chapter labeled "A Dynamic World" are intended to give us a taste of what was happening in the arts in a non-Western culture at the same time as the topics in the chapter occurred in the West. Although these boxes are brief, and to some may appear tokenistic, they remind us that there is a world beyond the Western one, and they give us another chance to apply our skills of perception and analysis. The artworks in the box may be similar to or quite different from the style of their Western counterparts. How they are similar or different is a question we should attempt to answer—using only the evidence of the art itself and the descriptive terminology we studied earlier in this section. The works of art in the Dynamic World boxes do have a relationship to the art of the chapter, and we should take the time to understand that relationship.

Maps and Timelines

Maps and timelines appear, mostly, at the beginning of each chapter. They contain information to help locate and correlate the art, history, philosophy, geography, etc. covered in the chapter. They also can be used to relate one chapter to another in time and place.

Chapter Opener

The opening pages of each chapter prepare you for what lies ahead. Firstly, an outline of the chapter is given, followed by key terms and definitions that will help you to understand the material covered. A short essay connects ideas and issues in the chapter with today's problems and circumstances.

How Art Works

At the beginning of each chapter, a feature page occurs, entitled "How Art Works," that discusses and illustrates a basic concept about art in general. Taken in total, these features present considerable, and important, information that helps us to understand what we can find in works of art. The result is that we possess fundamentals to increase our understanding about art and our confidence in approaching, analyzing, understanding, and relating to it.

Chapter Review

At the end of each chapter a Chapter Review box helps you connect the information you have just studied. The Critical Thought section stimulates your critical thinking about material in the chapter, again tying it to today's themes and concerns. The Summary prompts your comprehension with statements concerning what you should be able to do, having studied the chapter. Each box ends with a directive for you to practice your use of terminology and understanding of concepts by comparing works of art.

Cybersources and Examples

Throughout the text and at the end of each chapter are web addresses for additional examples and further study.

With regard to URLs for connecting to the World Wide Web, however, a warning is necessary. First, things change. A website active when this book went to press may no longer exist. (Wherever possible, works from major museums have been chosen, and those websites should remain active or should be accessible by finding the museum's home page through a standard search engine. Then, using the "collection" option will lead to an index from which the artist and work can be accessed.) Second, an initial attempt to link to a site may prove unsuccessful: "Unable to connect to remote host." A rule of thumb is to try to connect to the site three successive times before trying another URL. Be careful to type the URL exactly. Any incorrect character will cause the connection to fail (capital letters matter).

In addition to the specific web addresses listed in the text, some general sites can provide a wealth of additional information. An easy and vast reference for visual art and architecture is the Artcyclopedia at http://www.artcyclopedia.com/index.html. Here, individual artists can be referenced along with their artworks, as can searching by style, medium, subject, and nationality. A good architectural archive is "Mary Ann Sullivan's Digital Imaging Project" at http://www.bluffton.edu/~sullivanm/index/index2html#P although this site is among the redirects located in the Artcyclopedia just mentioned. "Art History Resources on the Net," http://libweb.sdsu.edu/sub_libs/cfields/art.html provides many useful hyperlinks.

Understanding and Evaluating the Arts

PUTTING THE ARTS IN CONTEXT

For centuries, scholars, philosophers, and aestheticians have debated without general resolution a definition of "art." The challenging range of arguments encompasses, among other considerations, opposing points of view that insist on one hand that "art" must meet a criterion of functionality—that is, be of some societal use—and, on the other hand, that "art" exists for its own sake. Our purpose in this text is to survey rather than dispute. Thus, in these pages, we will not solve the dilemma of art's definition, despite the energizing effect that such a discussion might engender. We can, however, examine some characteristics of the arts that will enhance our understanding.

Art has and has had profound effect on the quality of human life, as the pages of this text will assist us to understand, and its study requires seriousness of purpose. Having said that, however, we must be careful not to confuse seriousness of purpose in the study of art with a sweeping sanctification of works of art. Some art is serious, some art is profound, and some art is highly sacred. On the other hand, some art is light; some humorous; and some downright silly, superficial, and self-serving for its artists. Which is which may be debatable, but eventually we will desire to make judgments, and once again this text will help sort out the details.

The remainder of this section—that is, "Putting The Arts In Context"—treats four general subjects: (1) *The Arts and Ways of Knowing*, (2) *What Concerns Art?* (3) *The Functions of Art*, and (4) *Evaluating Works of Art*.

THE ARTS AND WAYS OF KNOWING

Humans are a creative species. Whether in science, politics, business, technology, or the arts, we depend on our creativity almost as much as anything else to meet the demands of daily life. Any book about the arts is a story about us: our perceptions of the world as we have come to see and respond to it and the ways we have communicated our understandings to each other since the Ice Age, more than 35,000 years ago (see Fig. **1.7**, Cave chamber at Lascaux).

Our study in this text will focus on vocabulary and perception, as well as on history. First, however, we need to have an overview of where the arts fall within the general scope of human endeavor.

As we begin this text, learning more about our humanness through art, let us start where we are. That means two things. First, it means relying on the perceptive capabilities we already have. Applying our current abilities to perceive will develop confidence in approaching works of art. Second, starting where we are means learning how art fits into the general scheme of the way people examine, communicate, and respond to the world around them. A course in the arts, designed to fulfill a requirement for a specified curriculum, means that the arts fit into an academic context that separates the way people acquire knowledge. Consequently, our first step in this exploration of the arts will be to place them in some kind of relationship with other categories of knowledge. Visual art, architecture, music, theatre, dance, and film belong in a broad category of pursuit called the "humanities," and that is where we begin.

The humanities, as opposed, for example, to the sciences, can very broadly be defined as those aspects of culture that look into what it means to be human. The sciences seek essentially to describe reality whereas the humanities seek to express humankind's subjective experiences of reality, to interpret reality, to transform our interior experience into tangible forms, and to comment upon reality, to judge and evaluate. But despite our desire to categorize, there really are few clear boundaries between the humanities and the sciences. The basic difference lies in the approach that separates investigation of the natural universe, technology, and social science from the search for truth about the universe undertaken by artists.

Within the educational system, the humanities traditionally have included the fine arts (painting, sculpture, architecture, music, theatre, dance, and cinema), literature, philosophy, and, sometimes, history. These subjects are all oriented toward exploring what it is to be human, what human beings think and feel, what motivates their actions and shapes their thoughts.

In addition, change in the arts differs from change in the sciences, for example, in one significant way: new scientific discovery and technology usually displaces the old; but new art does not invalidate earlier human expression. Obviously, not all artistic approaches survive, but the art of Picasso cannot make the art of Rembrandt a curiosity of history the way that the theories of Einstein did the views of William Paley. Nonetheless, much about art has changed over the centuries. Using a spectrum developed by Susan Lacy in *Mapping the Terrain: New Genre Public Art* (1995), we learn that at one time an artist may be an *experiencer*; at another, a *reporter*; at another, an *analyst*; and at still another time, an *activist*. Further, the nature of how art historians see art has changed over the centuries—for example, today we do not credit an artist's biography with all of the motivations for his or her work; and we now include works of art from previously marginalized groups such as women and minorities. These shifts in the disciplines of arts history itself are important considerations as we begin to understand the nature of art.

WHAT CONCERNS ART?

Among other concerns, art has typically concerned creativity, aesthetic communication, symbols, and the fine arts and crafts. Let's look briefly at each of these.

Creativity

Art has always evidenced a concern for creativity—that is, bringing forth new forces and forms that cause change. How this functions is subject for further debate. Nonetheless, something happens in which humankind takes chaos, formlessness, vagueness, and/or the unknown and crystallizes them into forms, designs, inventions, and ideas. Creativity underlies our existence. For example, creativity allows scientists to intuit that there is a possible path to a cure for cancer, for example, or to invent a computer. The same process allows artists to find new ways to express ideas through processes in which creative action, thought, material, and technique combine to create something new, and that "new thing," without words, triggers human experience—that is, our response to the artwork. Creativity lets Peter Paul Rubens find a way to express sacred ideas in complex forms, lines, and colors (Figs **13.11** and **13.12**), different from his Renaissance predecessors like Michelangelo (Chapter 11).

In the midst of this creative process is the art medium. Although most people can readily acknowledge the traditional media—for example, painting, traditional sculpture, and printmaking—sometimes an artwork does not conform to expectations or experiences—for example, a gigantic installation in two parts, of blue and yellow umbrellas (Fig. **18.24**).

Aesthetic Communication

Art usually involves communication. A common factor in art is a humanizing experience. Arguably, artists need other people with whom they can share their perceptions. When artworks and humans interact, many possibilities exist. Interaction may be casual and fleeting, as in the first meeting of two people, when one or both are not at all interested in each other. Similarly, an artist may not have much to say, or may not say it very well. For example, a poorly conceived and executed painting probably will not excite a viewer. Similarly, if a viewer is self-absorbed, distracted, unaware, has rigid preconceptions not met by the painting, or is so preoccupied by what may have occurred outside the museum that he or she finds it impossible to perceive what the artwork offers, then at least that part of the artistic experience fizzles. On the other hand, all conditions may be optimum, and a profoundly exciting and meaningful experience may occur: the painting may treat a significant subject in a unique manner, the painter's skill in manipulating the medium may be excellent, and the viewer may be receptive. Or the interaction may fall somewhere between these two extremes. In any case, the experience is a human one, and that is fundamental to art.

Throughout history, artistic communication has involved *aesthetics*. Aesthetics is the study of the nature of beauty and of art and comprises one of the five classical fields of philosophical inquiry—along with epistemology (the nature and origin of knowledge), ethics (the general nature of morals and of the specific moral choices to be made by the individual in relationship with others), logic (the principles of reasoning), and metaphysics (the nature of first principles and problems of ultimate reality). The term "aesthetics" (from the Greek for "sense perception") was coined by German philosopher Alexander Baumgarten in the mid-eighteenth century, but interest in what constitutes the beautiful and in the relationship between art and nature goes back at least to Plato and Aristotle, who saw art as *imitation* and beauty as the expression of a universal quality. In the late eighteenth century, the philosopher Immanuel Kant revolutionized aesthetics in his *Critique of Judgment* (1790) by viewing aesthetic appreciation not simply as the perception of intrinsic beauty, but as involving a judgment—subjective, but informed. Since Kant, the primary focus of aesthetics has shifted from the consideration of beauty *per se* to the nature of the artist, the role of art, and the relationship between the viewer and the work of art.

Symbols

Art is also concerned with symbols. Symbols are things that represent something else. They often use a material object to suggest something less tangible or less obvious: a wedding ring, for example. Symbols differ from signs, which suggest a fact or condition. Signs are what they denote. Symbols carry deeper, wider, and richer meanings. Look at Fig 0.14. Some people might identify this figure as a sign, which looks like a plus sign in arithmetic. But the figure might also be seen as a Greek cross, in which case it becomes a symbol because it suggests many images, meanings, and implications. Artworks use a variety of symbols in order to convey meaning. By using symbols, artworks can relay meanings that go well beyond the surface of the work and offer glimpses of the human condition that cannot be sufficiently described in any other manner. Symbols make artworks into doorways leading to enriched meaning. (See the discussion of symbolism in the "How Art Works" feature beginning Chapter 5, p. 142.)

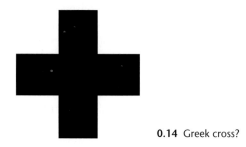

0.14 Greek cross?

Fine and Applied Art

One last consideration in our movement toward understanding what art concerns involves the difference between the terms "fine art" and "applied art." The "fine arts"—generally meaning painting, sculpture, and architecture—are prized for their purely aesthetic qualities. The terms "applied art" and "decorative arts" are used to describe art forms that have a primarily decorative rather than expressive or emotional purpose. The applied arts may include architecture. The decorative arts include handicrafts by skilled artisans, for example ornamental work in metal, stone, wood, and glass as well as textiles, pottery, and bookbinding. The term may also encompass aspects of interior design. In addition, personal objects such as jewelry, weaponry, tools, and costumes are considered to be part of the decorative arts. The term may extend, as well, to mechanical appliances and other products of industrial design. The term "decorative art" first appeared in 1791. Many decorative arts, such as weaving, basketry, or pottery, are also commonly considered to be "crafts," but the definitions of the terms are somewhat arbitrary and without sharp distinction.

THE FUNCTIONS OF ART

Art can function in many different ways: as *entertainment*, as *political or social weapon*, as *therapy*, and as *artifact*. One function is no more important than the others. Nor are they mutually exclusive: a single artwork can pursue any or all of them. Nor are these the only functions of art. Rather, they serve as indicators of how art has functioned in the past, and how it can function in the present. Like the types and styles of art we will examine later in the book, these four functions are options for artists and depend on what artists wish to do with their artworks.

Entertainment

Plays, paintings, concerts, and so on can provide escape from everyday cares, treat us to a pleasant time, and engage us in social occasions; they entertain us. They also give us insights into our hopes and dreams, likes and dislikes, as well as other cultures; and we can find healing therapy in entertainment.

The function of any one artwork depends on us. An artwork in which one person finds only entertainment may function as a social and personal comment for someone else. A Mozart (pronounced MOHT-sahrt) symphony, for example, can relax us, but it may also comment on the life of the composer and/or the conditions of eighteenth-century Austria.

Political and Social Commentary

When art seeks to bring about political change or to modify the behavior of large groups of people, it has political or social functions. In ancient Rome, for example, the authorities used music and theatre to keep masses of people occupied in order to quell urban unrest. On the other hand, Roman playwrights used their plays to attack incompetent or corrupt officials. The Greek playwright Aristophanes used comedy in such plays as *The Birds* to attack the political ideas of the leaders of fourth-century B.C.E.

Athenian society. In *Lysistrata* he attacked war by creating a story in which all the women of Athens go on a sex strike until Athens is rid of war and warmongers.

In late nineteenth-century Norway, Henrik Ibsen (IB-suhn) used his play *An Enemy of the People* (1882) as a platform for airing the issue of whether a government should ignore pollution in order to protect jobs or industry. In the United States at the turn of the twenty-first century, many artworks advance social and political causes and sensitize viewers, listeners, or readers to particular cultural situations.

Therapy

As therapy, art can help treat a variety of illnesses, both physical and mental. Role-playing, for example, frequently acts as a counseling tool in treating dysfunctional family situations. In this context, often called psychodrama, mentally ill patients act out their personal circumstances in order to find and cure the cause of their illness. The focus of this use of art as therapy is the individual. However, art in a much broader context acts as a healing agent for society's general illnesses as well. Artworks can illustrate society's failings and excesses in hopes of saving us from disaster. The laughter caused by comedy releases endorphins, chemicals produced by the brain, which strengthen the immune system.

Artifact

Art also functions as an artifact: a product that represents the ideas and technology of time and place. Artifacts, such as plays, paintings, poems, and buildings, connect us to our past. In this text, the function of art as artifact—as an example of a particular culture—takes on a central role.

When we examine art in the context of cultural artifact, one of the issues we face is the use of artworks in religious ritual. We could consider ritual as a separate function of art. Although we may not think of religious ritual as "art," in the broad context we have adopted for this text ritual often meets our definition of human communication using an artistic medium. Music, for example, when part of a religious ceremony, meets the definition, and theatre—if seen as an occasion planned and intended for presentation—would include religious rituals as well as events that take place in playhouses. Often, it is difficult to discern when ritual stops and secular production starts—for example, ancient Greek tragedy seems clearly to have evolved from ritual. When ritual, planned and intended for presentation, uses traditionally artistic media like music, dance, and theatre, we can study it as "art" and artifact of its particular culture.

EVALUATING WORKS OF ART

One of the questions everyone seems to ask about an artwork is, "Is it any good?" Whether it is rock music, a film, a play, a painting, or a classical symphony, judgments about the quality of a work often vary from one extreme to the other, ranging from "I liked it" and "It was interesting," to specific reasons why the artwork is thought to be effective or ineffective.

Criticism should be a detailed process of analysis to gain understanding and appreciation. Identifying the formal elements of an artwork—learning what to look for—is the first step. We describe an artwork by examining its many facets and then try to understand how they work together to create meaning or experience. We then try to state what that meaning or experience is. Only when that process is complete should we attempt judgment.

Value judgments are intensely personal, and some opinions are more informed than others, thus representing more authoritative judgments. However, disagreements about quality can actually enhance, rather than confuse, the experience of a work of art if they result in an examination about why the differences might exist. In this way, we develop a deeper understanding of the artwork. Nonetheless, criticism may be exercised without involving any value judgment whatsoever—and this is the point. We can thoroughly analyze and dissect any work of art and describe what it comprises without making value judgments. For example, we can describe and analyze line, color, mass, balance, texture, composition, and/or message. We can observe how all these factors affect people and their responses. We can spend significant amounts of time and write at considerable length in such a process and never pass a value judgment at all.

Does this discussion mean all artworks are equal in value? Not at all. It means that in order to understand what criticism involves, we must separate descriptive analysis, which can be satisfying in and of itself, from the act of passing value judgments. We may not like the work we have analyzed, but we may have understood something we did not understand before. Passing judgment may play no role whatsoever in our understanding of an artwork. But we are still involved in criticism.

As an exercise in understanding, criticism is necessary. We must investigate and describe. We must experience the need to know enough about the process, product, and experience of art if we are to have perceptions that mean anything worthwhile to ourselves and if we are to have perceptions to share with others.

Types of Criticism

There are a number of ways to "criticize" or analyze works of art. Some are fairly straightforward, and some are relatively complex and theoretically involved. Let's begin with two *basic* types of criticism. These are *formal* criticism and *contextual* criticism. Once we have these concepts in hand, we can branch out a little to examine the theoretically involved and opposing critical theories of *structuralism* and *deconstruction*.

Formal Criticism

Formal criticism is an analysis applying no external conditions or information. The artwork is analyzed according to style, composition—elements of line, form, color, balance—technique, melody, harmony, and so forth. Formal criticism approaches the artwork solely as an entity within itself and explains how the artist has taken these basic qualities and used them to build the work—how the employment of elements reveals style and makes the work affect the respondent. In so doing, we would develop a rather lengthy formal analysis of this artwork. In doing this, however, we would remain in our description and analysis strictly within the frame, so to speak. In other words, all of the conclusions we would reach about the work would come solely from evidence that exists in the work. In this formal approach, external information—about the artist, the times, the story behind the work, and so on—is irrelevant. Consequently, the formal approach helps us analyze how an artwork operates and helps us decide why the artwork produces the response it does. Formal criticism is exemplified by the work of the "New Critics" such as Allen Tate (1899–1979), who insisted on the intrinsic value of a work of art and focused attention on the work alone as an independent unit of meaning. As an example, we will do a brief analysis of Molière's (mohl-YAIR) comedy *Tartuffe* (tahr-TOOF; 1664):

Orgon, a rich bourgeois, has allowed a religious conman, Tartuffe, to gain complete hold over him. Tartuffe has moved into Orgon's house and tries to seduce Orgon's wife at the same time that he is planning to marry Orgon's daughter. Tartuffe is unmasked, and Orgon orders him out. Tartuffe seeks his revenge by claiming title to Orgon's house and blackmailing him with some secret papers. At the very last instant, Tartuffe's plans are foiled by the intervention of the king, and the play ends happily.

We have just described a story. Were we to go one step further and analyze the plot, we would look, among other things, for points at which *crises* occur and cause the characters to make important decisions; we would also want to know how those decisions moved the play from one point to the next. In addition, we would try to locate the extreme crisis—the *climax*. Meanwhile, we would discover auxiliary parts of the plot such as reversals: for example, when Tartuffe is discovered and the characters become aware of the true situation. Depending on how detailed our criticism were to become, we could work our way through each and every aspect of the plot. We might then devote some time to describing and analyzing the driving force—the character—of each person in the play and how the characters relate to each other. Has Molière created fully developed characters? Are they types, or do they seem to behave more or less like real individuals? In examining meaning, we would no doubt conclude that the play deals with religious hypocrisy, and that Molière had a particular point of view on that subject. In this approach, information about the playwright, previous performances, historic relationships, and so on is irrelevant.

Contextual Criticism

On the other hand, contextual criticism seeks meaning by examining related information "outside" the artwork, such as the artist's life, his or her culture, social, and political conditions and philosophies, public and critical reactions to the work, and so on. These can all be researched and applied to the work in order to enhance perception and understanding. This approach tends to view the artwork as an artifact generated from particular contextual needs, conditions, and/or attitudes. If we carry our criticism of *Tartuffe* in this direction, we would note that certain historical events help to clarify the play. For example, the object of Molière's attention probably was the Company of the Holy Sacrament, a secret, conspiratorial, and influential society in France at the time. Like many fanatical religious sects—including those of our own time—the society sought to enforce its own view of morality by spying on the lives of others and seeking out heresies, in this case, in the Roman Catholic Church. Its followers were religious fanatics, and they had a considerable effect on the lives of the citizenry at large. If we were to follow this path of criticism, any and all such contextual matters that might illuminate or clarify what happens in the play would be pursued.

Structuralism

Structuralism applies to the artwork a broader significance, insisting that individual phenomena—in this case artworks—can be understood *only* within the context of the overall structures of which they are a part. These structures represent universal sets of relationships that derive meaning from their contrasts and interactions within a specific context. Structuralist criticism, associated with Roland Barthes (BAHR-tuh; 1915–1980), derives by analogy from structural linguistics, which sees a "text" as a system of signs whose meaning is derived from the pattern of their interactions rather than from any external reference. This approach opposes critical positions that seek to determine an artist's intent, for example. Thus, the meaning of a work of art lies not in what the artist may have had in mind, but in the patterns of contextual relationships that work within the artwork. Finally, structuralism also opposes approaches, such as *deconstruction*, which deny the existence of uniform patterns and definite meanings.

Deconstruction

Deconstruction, associated with the French philosopher Jacques Derrida (dare-ee-DAH; b. 1930), was also originally associated with literary criticism, but has been applied to other disciplines. Derrida used the term "text," for example, to include any subject to which critical analysis can be applied. Deconstructing something means "taking it apart." The process of deconstruction implies drawing out all the threads of a work to identify its multitude of possible meanings, and, on the other hand, undoing the "constructs" of ideology or convention that have imposed meaning on the work. All of which leads to the conclusion that there is no such thing as a single meaning in a work of art, nor can it claim any absolute truth. Inasmuch as a work can outlast its author, its meanings transcend any original intentions. In other words, the viewer brings as much to the work as the artist, and, thus, there are no facts, only interpretations. The details of an artwork become only a sidebar to the interpretation that we, as viewers, bring to it based on our own experiences and circumstances.

Making Judgments

Now that we have defined criticism and noted two approaches we might take in pursuing it, we can move on to the final step—making value judgments.

There are several approaches to the act of judgment. Two characteristics, however, apply to all artworks: they are *crafted*, and they *communicate* something to us about our experiences as humans. Making a judgment about the quality of an artwork should address each of these.

Artisanship

Judging a work's artisanship means judging how it is crafted or made. Generally, such judgments require knowledge about the medium of the artwork. It is, for example, difficult to judge how a musical symphony is crafted without having some knowledge of musical composition. The same may be said of judging how well a painting, sculpture, building, or play is made. Nonetheless, some criteria exist that allow general judgment of works of art. These criteria include *clarity* and *interest*.

Applying the standard of clarity means deciding if the work has coherence. Even the most complex works of art need some handle that allows us to approach them and begin to understand how they work. This standard of judgment has stood the test of time. Artworks have been compared to onions in that the well made ones allow respondents to peel away translucent layers, with each layer taking us closer to the core. Some people are able to peel away all the layers, and some people are able to peel away only one or two, but a masterfully crafted work of art will have a coherence that allows a grasp on even the very surface layer.

Applying the standard of interest is similar to applying the standard of clarity in that there are layers of devices or qualities that artists use to capture and hold our interest. Masterfully crafted works of art employ such devices and qualities. Three such qualities are (1) universality (the artist's ability to touch a common experience or feeling within us), (2) carefully developed structures or focal points that lead us where the artist intends us to go, and (3) freshness of approach that makes us curious to investigate further. When we watch a tired and trite mystery, we know what is going to happen, the characters are stale clichés, and we lose interest almost immediately. A masterfully crafted work will hold us—even if we know the story. Such is the case with plays like Sophocles' Oedipus the King or Shakespeare's Hamlet.

If a work of art does not appear clear or interesting, we may wish to examine whether the fault lies in the work or in ourselves before rendering judgment.

Communication

Evaluating what an artwork is trying to say offers more immediate opportunity for judgment and less need for expertise. Johann Wolfgang von Goethe (GUR-te), the nineteenth-century poet, novelist, and playwright, set out a basic, commonsense approach to communication. Because it provides an organized means for discovering an artwork's communication by progressing from analytical to judgmental functions, Goethe's approach is a helpful way in which to end our discussion on criticism. Goethe posed three questions: What is the artist trying to say? Does he or she succeed? Was the artwork worth the effort? These questions focus on the artist's communication by making us identify, first, what was being attempted and, second, the artist's success in that attempt. Whether or not the project was worth the effort asks us to decide if the communication was important. Was it worthwhile?